Parent's Page

MW01045491

In the Declaration of Independence, Jefferson wrote, "all men are created equal." Though the deeper sentiment is true, at face value this is overly simplistic. If we compare any two people we notice that they are far from equal. We differ in talent, strength, appearance, health, opportunity, and just about everything! Therefore, the question isn't whether or not people are equal, but rather: what differences matter and how do we treat people with differences?

This is where fairness comes in. Fairness is putting aside our biases in order to avoid partiality based on unsubstantial factors. The goal of fairness is justice, the concept of things being placed in the appropriate position according to Godly standards, even if it doesn't always *seem* fair.

For example, when we see Allah's (SWT) differentiated blessings to people, we might feel that it is unfair. Why don't I get a new backpack? Why am I bad at sports? Our first lesson teaches that whenever we feel that things are "unfair," we must look at things from another perspective: if two people are treated differently, that doesn't mean that it is unfair. Building empathy helps us understand that to truly be fair, people must be treated according to their own, unique, circumstances. Asad learns this in our first story, *"Finding Fairness,"* as he struggles to accept his grade from Mr. Salmaan.

Our second lesson is that we have a responsibility to act fairly in our social interactions, even if it means going against our own interests. Allah (SWT) says, "Stand firmly for justice, though it may be against your own selves or your parents or near relatives" (4:135). If we do not, imbalance and disharmony would ensue. In our second story, *"Acting Fairly,"* Amira realizes that Shireen must be fair in choosing people to act in the class play, not giving Amira the part simply because she is her friend.

Credits & Honors
Creative Developers: Maryum Mohsin
                              & Kenneth Molloy
Art Director: Annie Idris
Editors: Amin Aaser & Sana Aaser
Researcher: Armaan Siddiqi

FINDING FAIRNESS

Mr. Salmaan returns graded book reports to the class.

Asad's report has a silver star on it.

Asad asks Mr. Salmaan about the assignment.

Mr. Salmaan, why didn't I get a gold star?

I expect more of you, Asad. You can do better.

Frustrated, Asad returns to his seat.

More?! Better?

On the way home, Asad complains to Mom.

Mr. Salmaan said he expects more of me.

He should treat us the same! It's not fair!

In her car seat, Yusra cries loudly.

Later that evening, Mom makes Asad's favorite dinner—burgers.

Asad sits at the table.

Why is there baby food on my plate?

Asad grumbles to himself but eats the mashed carrots and potatoes.

After dinner, in the family room, Mom takes out blocks for Asad and Yusra to play with.

Yusra chews on a block.

Finally, it's time for bed. Asad brushes his teeth, does his wudu', and goes to his room.

I've set out your pajamas.

Asad picks up the pajamas.

What? These are baby pajamas. And not just that, they are *girl's* pajamas!

Well, you wanted me to treat you and Yusra the same...

But, I don't want to be treated the same anymore. I'm different!

Asad throws himself on the bed and covers his head with his pillow.

Mom sits on the side of the bed.

Asad rolls onto his back.

Mom hugs Asad close.

Questions:

1. Why does Mom treat Asad and Yusra the same?

2. What does being fair mean?

3. If Allah (SWT) doesn't treat us all the same, is He still being fair?

Chocolate Baklava Roll-Ups

Serves ten people

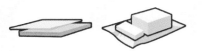
30 pieces Phyllo Pastry squares, 6x6 in

3/4 cup melted butter

1 cup of honey

3/4 cup cocoa powder

juice of 1 lemon

1/2 tsp of rose water

crushed nuts

1. Preheat the oven to 350°F.

2. Mix honey, rose water, and lemon juice.

3. Spread a pastry square on a flat plate. Brush with butter all over.

4. Spread a little honey syrup and cocoa powder over it.

5. Layer another sheet over it and repeat the process 3 times.

6. Sprinkle nuts over the last layer.

7. Start rolling from one end to the other as tightly as possible.

8. Brush all over lightly with butter.

9. Place on a greased, oven-proof tray, seam side down.

10. Bake for 10 minutes.

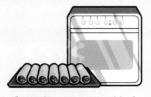
11. Turn them over and bake for another 10 minutes.

12. Serve with chocolate syrup, honey, or golden syrup.

*Adapted from www.foodaholic.biz

The Sweet Taste of Fairness

In the Qur'an

إِنَّ اللَّهَ يَأْمُرُ
بِالْعَدْلِ
وَالْإِحْسَانِ

Allah orders justice
and fairness.
(Surah An-Nahl, Ayah 90)

What does it mean if something is fair?
Let's answer this question through an activity!

You will need 12 raisins to help you count.
Follow the instructions and questions below.

Amin has five raisins and you only have one.

Count out the raisins and put them in the boxes
to show how many raisins Amin and you each have.

Amin's Box

Now, do the activity again,
but this time, you start with
five raisins and
Amin only has one.

Mr. Salmaan has four extra raisins. He gives Amin and you each an equal number of raisins.

Count out four more raisins. Now put them in the boxes to show how many raisins Amin and you would have if Mr. Salmaan gives each of you the same number (two each).

Is it fair? How many raisins do you each have? How can you make it fair (so that each of you has five raisins)?

Your Box

Mr. Salmaan's class is learning about theater. Shireen is the director of the class play.

Back in her desk, Shireen tries to get Amira's attention.

Amira wants Shireen to pick her for the lead role.

The time for auditions arrives. One after another, each student reads lines from the play, showcasing their best acting skills.

Shireen scores each performance in her notebook.

Amira performs well. As she leaves the stage, she whispers to Shireen.

Sarah also auditions.
She performs even better.

Shireen doesn't know what to do.
She has to make a choice.

Questions :

1. Should Shireen select Sarah or Amira for the lead role? Why?

2. Why does it matter who Shireen chooses?

3. Have you ever had to make a difficult choice like this?

At the end of the auditions, the performers come back to the auditorium.

It doesn't feel right, but I can't disappoint my friend.

The lead role will go to... Amira.

Yay!

Thanks Shireen. I'll be the best lead ever!

I was hoping you could do me a favor...

Sorry, I don't have time to help you, Shireen. I need to practice my lines.

The first day of rehearsal is a disaster. The set isn't ready and Amira keeps forgetting her lines.

The second day of rehearsal is not much better.

The third day of rehearsal is just as bad.

The next day, Amira overhears two others.

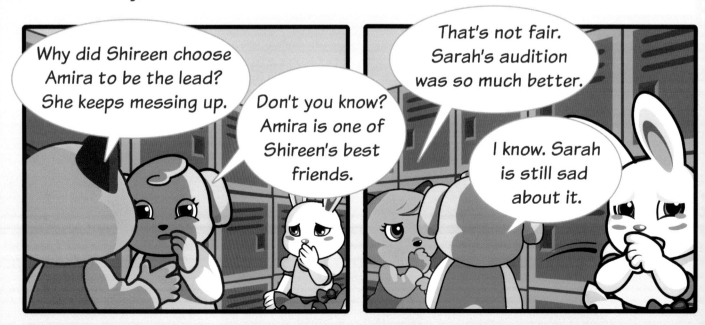

Amira realizes that she pressured Shireen to choose her.

Oh no! What have I done?

Shireen, can I ask you something?

Yeah...sure.

Did you pick me for the part because I'm your friend or because I had the best audition?

Umm...well...I knew you wanted the lead role so bad, and...

Shireen, I was wrong to pressure you.

99 Names of ALLAH

THE FAIR ONE

اَلْـمُـقْـسِـطُ

Al - Muqsit

Riddles

Why did Amin invite all of his friends to the park?

It was the county fair.

What is the nicest ride at the amusement park?

The Fair-is wheel.

What are nice bedtime stories?

Fair-y tales.

How should you play hopscotch?

Fair and square.